THINKology

ENGAGING ACTIVITIES

TO ENHANCE THE CREATIVE MIND

by
Nathan Levy and Scott Hobson

Copyright © 2012
All rights reserved.
No part of this book may be reproduced in any form without permission in writing from the publisher.

Nathan Levy Books, LLC

18 Moorland Blvd.

Monroe Township, NJ 08831

Phone: 732-605-1643

Fax: 732-656-7822

www.storieswithholes.com

ISBN 9781878347718

Nathan Levy's Brain Building Activity Book:

Thinkology

The suffix "ology" means the theory and study behind a particular subject. Thinkology provides activities that can take creative thinking and writing to the next level. By using activities that focus on imagination, humor, and brainpower, children begin to gain a greater understanding of creative thinking and writing. Teachers and parents will find inspiring and thought-provoking activities ranging in scope from when students first experienced prejudice, to creating their own original stories. This book provides unique and interesting ways to further the "ology" of creative thought and written expression – assuring integrated thinking across all subjects areas – language arts, science, math, social studies, gifted and special education. Activities are appropriate for thinkers from the crib to college. Thinkology enhances valuable critical thinking skills for all ages!

Happy Thinking,
Nathan Levy & Scott Hobson

About the Authors

Nathan Levy

Nathan Levy is the author of more than 40 books which have sold over 300,000 copies to teachers and parents in the United States, Europe, Asia, South America, Australia and Africa. His unique Stories with Holes series continues to be proclaimed the most popular activity used in gifted, special education and regular classrooms by hundreds of educators. An extremely popular, dynamic speaker on thinking, writing and differentiation, Nathan is in high demand as a workshop leader in school and business settings. He has worked as a school principal, district supervisor, gifted coordinator, is a company president and management trainer, as well as, the father of four daughters. Nathan's ability to transfer knowledge and strategies to audiences through humorous, thought provoking stories assures that participants leave with a plethora of new ways to approach their future endeavors.

Scott Hobson

Scott Hobson is an educational consultant, speaker and author who has presented high quality workshops to educators and parents at conferences at the national, state and local levels. With over 20 years of experience in education, Mr. Hobson has served as Principal, Assistant Principal, and Master Teacher. Scott has mentored aspiring administrators, as well as trained teachers and parents in better ways to help children learn. Scott has developed unique teaching strategies that connect critical thinking, writing and the love of learning all for the purpose of enhancing student performance and accountability. His background and experience have helped him produce five books: Breakfast for the Brain, Principles of Fearless Leadership, Affective Cognitive Thinking, Thinkology, and Miss Miller's Special Valentine.

Table of Contents

Introduction 2
About The Authors 3
Activity 1: Rush Hour 9
Activity 2: From Me To You 10
Activity 3: Guided Tour 11
Activity 4: I Quit 12
Activity 5: I Give Up 13
Activity 6: Bite Your Tongue 14
Activity 7: Split Personality 15
Activity 8: Makes Sense To Me 16
Activity 9: Makes Sense To Me Too 17
Activity 10: Reflections 18
Activity 11: No Way 19
Activity 12: Something Special 20
Activity 13: Putting It To The Test 21
Activity 14: Color Blind 22
Activity 15: Abracadabra 23
Activity 16: Friendly Advice 24
Activity 17: Me Too 25
Activity 18: I've Got A Secret 26
Activity 19: My Best Friend 27
Activity 20: You Don't Know Anything 28
Activity 21: Don't Worry, Be Happy 29
Activity 22: Do You Hear What I Hear? 30
Activity 23: Wishful Thinking 31
Activity 24: Context Clues 32
Activity 25: Feelings 33
Activity 26: The World According To Me 34

Table of Contents

Activity 27: One Of A Kind 35
Activity 28: Too Cool For Words 36
Activity 29: My Bad 37
Activity 30: To Be Or Not To Be 38
Activity 31: Emotional Rescue 39
Activity 32: I Don't Feel Like 40
Activity 33: Do Your Part. 41
Activity 34: Tell Me How 42
Activity 35: Quizzical Questions #1 43
Activity 36: Quizzical Questions #2 44
Activity 37: Good News, Bad News 45
Activity 38: It Ain't Easy 46
Activity 39: It's All Relative 47
Activity 40: It Is What It Is 48
Activity 41: Helping Hands 49
Activity 42: The Best Laid Plans 50
Activity 43: Little Dilemmas 51
Activity 44: Personification 52
Activity 45: Conduct Yourself 53
Activity 46: A Profound Perception 54
Activity 47: Puzzles To Ponder #1 55
Activity 48: Puzzles To Ponder #2 56
Activity 49: Puzzles To Ponder #3 57
Activity 50: A Quick Query 58
Activity 51: Beginnings 59
Activity 52: Bon Appetite 60
Activity 53: Really Prime Number 61
Activity 54: A Family Affair 62

Table of Contents

Activity 55: Do It Yourself 63

Activity 56: Impending Amazement 64

Activity 57: What's The Point 65

Activity 58: Tell Me Why 66

Activity 59: Game On 67

Activity 60: Can I Quote You On That? 68

Activity 61: Imagine This 69

Activity 62: Show Time 70

Activity 63: Clichés 71

Activity 64: Rules and Regulations 72

Activity 65: You Can't Make Me 73

Activity 66: Home Sweet Home 74

Activity 67: Seasons Greetings 75

Activity 68: Hold Your Breath 76

Activity 69: Strange Magic 77

Activity 70: This And That 78

Tools of the Trade Activity Pages 81–94

Dynamic Workshops 95

Rush Hour

Activity 1

What is patience?

List three things for which you would be willing to wait.

1.

2.

3.

List three things for which you would not be willing to wait.

1.

2.

3.

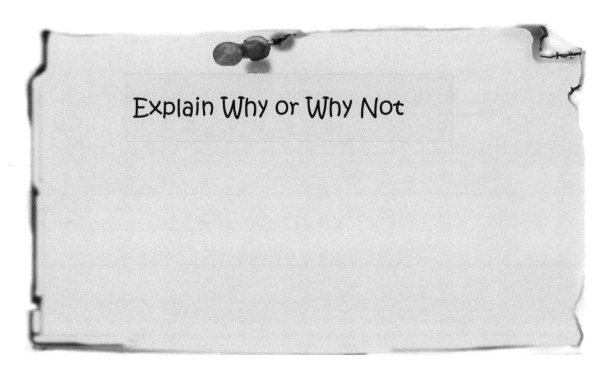

Explain Why or Why Not

Activity 2

From Me To You

Think About

- The most thoughtful/meaningful thing I ever did for anyone.
- The most thoughtful/meaningful thing anyone ever did for me.
- The most thoughtful/meaningful thing I ever did for myself.

Write a paragraph on any or all of them.

_____
_____
_____
_____
_____
_____

Be sure to include: Who was involved? What happened? Why did it happen? Where did it happen? Why was it thoughtful? What made it special? How did you feel... before and after?

_____
_____
_____
_____

Guided Tour

Activity 3

- In your mind visualize one of the following things in your life. Recall as many details about it as you can. Write a descriptive paragraph with the title: Guided Tour of My...

Choose one:
- Bedroom
- Refrigerator
- Brain
- School
- Neighborhood

_____
_____
_____
_____
_____
_____
_____

Draw a map to accompany your description. Be sure to point out all the interesting and unusual sights and highlights of this trip!

Activity 4

I Quit

Which would be harder for you to quit?

Using your cell phone or watching television?

   or

Texting or using your computer?

   or

Playing with your pet or playing video games?

   or

What are some things you cannot quit?

What are some things you wish you could quit?

Explain your reasoning.

I Give Up

Activity 5

List 5 things you <u>would rather</u> not give up.

1.

2.

3.

4.

5.

List 5 things you <u>could not</u> give up.

1.

2.

3.

4.

5.

Compare your lists. How are they similar/different?

Similar	Different

Activity 6

Bite Your Tongue

What would be easier for you to say?

You're right ☐   I'm wrong ☐

I give up ☐   You win ☐

You win ☐   I lose ☐

Justify your choices and give reasons or examples:

_____
_____
_____
_____
_____

Split Personality

Activity 7

Describe a day of the week that is like your personality.
_____
_____

Describe a day of the week that is unlike your personality.
_____
_____

Describe a time of the day that is like your personality.
_____
_____

Describe a season that is like your personality.
_____
_____

Write about why you made these choices.
_____
_____
_____

Activity 8: Makes Sense to Me

Which would you least like to touch or feel?

-A Cactus or Embarrassment?

 or

Which would you least like to eat?

-Worm juice or crow?

 or

Which would you least like to see?

-Your favorite team lose
or
your friend cry?

 or

Which would you least like to hear?

- Fingernails on a chalkboard
or
Someone's heart break?

 or

Explain your answers.

_____
_____

Makes Sense to Me Too!

Activity 9

Create your own list of leasts and accompanying comparisons.

Which would you least like to touch or feel?

_____ or _____

Which would you least like to taste or eat?

_____ or _____

Which would you least like to see?

_____ or _____

Which would you least like to hear?

_____ or _____

Compare your "leasts" with someone else. How are they alike and different?

_____
_____
_____
_____

Activity 10

Reflections

Take your teacher's point of view and answer the question.

What are you like to teach?

In your mind pretend to interview your teacher and one other classmate. Your task is to figure out what kind of student you appear to be. Think about specific incidents, situations, or accomplishments. Use these events to help you draw some conclusions about their perspective of you. What did you learn about yourself?

Write your conclusions.

_____
_____
_____
_____
_____
_____
_____

Share your conclusions with them.

No Way

Activity 11

List three famous people you do not want to live near.

1. _____
2. _____
3. _____

OR

List three famous people you would like as neighbors.

1. _____
2. _____
3. _____

Choose one of the above and then explain your thinking in at least one paragraph.

Activity 12
Something Special

List five of your most prized possessions.

1. _____
2. _____
3. _____
4. _____
5. _____

Visualize then describe each one.

Explain what makes them valuable.

How would you keep them safe?

Where would you hide them?

Would you purchase insurance for them? Yes ☐ No ☐

Ideas: your baseball card collection or sense of humor?
Your favorite outfit or loyalty?
An award you won or compassion for others?
Your games or friendship?

Putting it to the Test

Activity 13

Do you object to standardized tests? Would you like to get rid of them? State something good or bad about tests.

_____
_____

If you didn't have exit exams, do you think you would work harder or not? How would your study habits change?

_____
_____

What advice would you give a friend before an important test?

_____
_____

What kind of tests do people have to face in life outside of school?

_____
_____

What are some alternatives to traditional exams? Suggest some ideas.

_____
_____

Activity 14

Color Blind

In a paragraph for each:

1. Write about what color best represents your mood when you are happy/sad/angry.

_____
_____
_____
_____

2. Write about something in your life that is/was colorful.

_____
_____
_____
_____

3. Write about something in your life that is/was bland.

_____
_____
_____
_____

Activity 15

Abracadabra

Pretend you are a magician.

Write about a person, place, and thing that you would like to make disappear.

_____
_____
_____

Write each in a separate paragraph. Give several reasons for your choices.

_____
_____
_____

Think about a time that you wish you could make yourself disappear.

_____
_____
_____

What happened to make you feel that way?

_____
_____
_____

Activity 16: Friendly Advice

Make a list of things you could do to get along better with...

- Your family
- Your teachers
- Your friends
- Your enemies

Take one of your lists and write a letter offering sound advice to yourself.

Dear,

Me Too

Activity 17

Would you like to be cloned? Why or why not?

_____
_____
_____
_____

What would be the best thing about it? The worst thing?

Best thing: _____

Worst thing: _____

Explain what you would have your clone do or not do for you.

_____
_____
_____
_____

Activity 18

I've Got a Secret

If your nemesis/enemy had an important secret and didn't want anyone to know about it, would you tell the secret to someone? _____

Would telling the secret be wrong? _____

Why or why not? _____
_____
_____
_____
_____
_____
_____

My Best Friend

Activity 19

List four famous people, living or dead, who you would like to have as a friend. In a paragraph explain your choices.

1. _____
   _____
   _____

2. _____
   _____
   _____

3. _____
   _____
   _____

4. _____
   _____
   _____

Activity 20: You Don't Know Anything

List three things that you think you know more about than your parents.

1. _____
2. _____
3. _____

Using ideas from your list write at least one paragraph about these things.

_____
_____
_____
_____
_____
_____
_____
_____
_____
_____
_____
_____
_____
_____

Don't Worry, Be Happy

Activity 21

What makes rich people happy?

_____
_____
_____

What makes poor people happy?

_____
_____
_____

What makes everyone happy?

_____
_____
_____

Make a chart or venn diagram to help explain your answer?

Activity 22: Do You Hear What I Hear?

The word "whatever" has been named the most annoying word in the english language.

What are words people use too often? _____
_____

What are words people do not use enough? _____
_____

What are words I find annoying? _____
_____

What are words I find soothing? _____
_____

Make a list of your favorite synonyms and antonyms.

1.

2.

3.

Wishful Thinking

Activity 23

A wizard has just granted you four wishes. Complete the following statements and then explain why.

I wish that I knew everything about _____
_____
_____
_____
_____
_____

I wish I could _____
_____
_____
_____
_____

I wish I never had _____
_____
_____
_____
_____
_____

I wish my pet _____ could _____
_____
_____
_____
_____
_____

Activity 24: Context Clues

Complete the following and explain:

What is your favorite word? _____
_____

What is your least favorite word? _____
_____

Make up a new word that describes you. _____
_____

Create a sentence for each of the words that demonstrates you know the meaning of all four words.

1. _____
2. _____
3. _____
4. _____

Feelings

Activity 25

Complete the following and explain:

1. I am happy for those who have…

   _____
   _____
   _____

2. I'm jealous/envious of those who have…

   _____
   _____
   _____

3. I wish that everyone had…

   _____
   _____
   _____

Activity 26
The World According to Me...

Finish these thoughts:
If I were in charge of the world I would...

Never _____

Help _____

Construct _____

Shout _____

Accept _____

PART 2

Avoid_____

Demolish _____

Whisper _____

Forbid _____

Choose 3 and write a paragraph for each.

_____
_____
_____

Follow up assignment:
Change world to Past, Present, Future

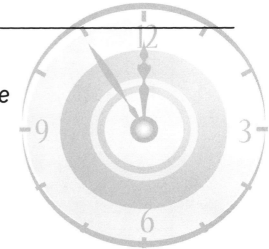

34

One of a Kind...

Activity 27

What are <u>three</u> of life's most unique objects? (ie. cell phones, super glue, Mona Lisa)

1. _____
2. _____
3. _____

In a paragraph, evaluate why each item is so unique and what led you to your choices.

_____
_____

AND

What are <u>three</u> of life's most common objects? (ie. cars, pens, colds...)

1. _____
2. _____
3. _____

Compare your lists: Which objects are more important? Is it better to be unique or common?

_____
_____

In a paragraph, evaluate why each item is common and what led you to your choices.

_____
_____

Activity 28: Too Cool for Words...

What makes you cool?.
_____
_____

Discuss outlook, fashion, etc...
_____
_____

What does the phrase "cool as the other side of the pillow" mean?
_____
_____

When can "cool" and "hot" mean the same thing?
_____
_____

When can "cool" be unfriendly? Give some examples.
_____
_____

Research the fashion from 3 different decades. Would you wear them? Why or why not?
_____
_____

My Bad...

Activity 29

Think about a time when you accidently broke something. Even though you did not do it on purpose, was it really your fault?

Convince someone that it wasn't your fault and then convince them that it was.

It <u>WAS</u> your fault.

_____
_____
_____
_____
_____
_____
_____

It <u>WAS NOT</u> your fault.

_____
_____
_____
_____
_____
_____
_____

Activity 30

To Be or Not to Be...

List 10 things that <u>could never happen</u> in the summer and/or winter and explain why.

1. _____ 6. _____
2. _____ 7. _____
3. _____ 8. _____
4. _____ 9. _____
5. _____ 10. _____

Draw a picture or cartoon of one of those impossibilities.

List 10 things that <u>could only happen</u> in the summer/winter and explain why.

1. _____ 6. _____
2. _____ 7. _____
3. _____ 8. _____
4. _____ 9. _____
5. _____ 10. _____

Emotional Rescue

Activity 31

What is the funniest thing that ever happened to you?
_____
_____

What is the most embarrassing thing that ever happened to you?
_____
_____

What is the craziest thing that has happened to you?
_____
_____

What is the most ironic thing that has happened to you?
_____
_____

Optional Activity: Create your own graphic novella to tell your story.

Activity 32

I Don't Feel Like...

Finish the statement and give three reasons.
I don't feel like...

_____
_____
_____

1. _____
_____
_____

2. _____
_____
_____

3. _____
_____
_____

Do Your Part

Activity 33

If you could do one thing for someone else, what would it be?

_____
_____
_____

If you could have someone else do something for you, what would it be?

_____
_____
_____

Explain your choices in a paragraph.

_____
_____
_____
_____
_____
_____

Activity 34

Tell Me How...

Answer two of the questions below. Use specific examples.

How can you hide from yourself?

_____
_____
_____
_____

OR

How can you lose and win at the same time?

_____
_____
_____
_____

OR

How can zero make nothing into something?

_____
_____
_____
_____

Quizzical Questions #1...

Activity 35

1. When is something better than nothing?
___
___
___
___

2. When is nothing better than something?
___
___
___
___

3. Make up a question that has no answer.
Be creative...use your imagination and sense of humor...
___
___
___
___

43

Activity 36

Quizzical Questions #2...

Answer each of the following questions:

What would you ask a fish, if the fish could only answer one question?
(Do you ever get tired of seafood?)

_____

_____

And

What would you wear if there were no rules?

_____

_____

And

If you could instantly learn something, what would it be?
Be creative...use your imagination and sense of humor...

_____

_____

Good News, Bad News...

Activity 37

Invent creative solutions to the following:

Pick one problem and write about how you would solve it.

1. Someone gave you 5 crates of apples, what do you do before they get rotten?

_____
_____
_____
_____

2. You work for an ice cream company and the freezer breaks down.

_____
_____
_____
_____

3. You won the lottery and only have 4 hours to claim your prize in Los Angeles. However, you are in New York City.

_____
_____
_____
_____

Activity 38

It Ain't Easy...

"It is hard to fail but it is worse never to have tried to succeed."

1. What does this quote mean? _____
_____

2. At what things have you failed? _____
_____

3. At what things have you succeeded? _____
_____

4. What would you like to try to do that you haven't done yet? _____

"Don't judge a book by its cover."

1. What does this quote mean? _____
_____

2. Name a book that you read that you did not expect to like, but loved. Why did you love it? _____
_____

3. When did you underestimate someone? _____
_____

4. When did someone underestimate you? _____
_____

It's All Relative...

Activity 39

How do you define "EXCEPTIONAL"?

1. Tell about something that is exceptional.

___

2. Tell about something that is less than exceptional.

___

3. What are some positive things about being exceptional?

___

4. Evaluate: What is exceptional about you?
(Consider appearance, athletic ability, intelligence, etc.)

___

Activity 40: It Is What It Is...

I'm sure you've heard the statement: Life isn't fair.

Tell about a time when this was true for you at school, home, playground, etc.

_____
_____
_____

Tell about a time when this was NOT true for you.

_____
_____
_____

Helping Hand...

Activity 41

Tell someone the best way to forget about a bad memory.

_____
_____
_____
_____
_____

OR

Tell someone the best way to eat an ice cream cone on a hot day.

_____
_____
_____
_____
_____

Activity 42
The Best Laid Plans...

There is a proposal in your town to turn a local mall into a park. The mall is one of two malls in town. It contains a lot of great stores, a movie theater and places to eat. The proposed park will have a huge playground, athletic fields and a fishing pond.

1. Brainstorm a list of "PROS" and "CONS" for keeping the mall or creating the park.

PROS	CONS
_____	_____
_____	_____
_____	_____
_____	_____

2. Choose a side.
_____

3. Write what you will do.
_____
_____

4. Prepare an argument to persuade others to agree with you.
_____
_____
_____
_____

Little Dilemmas...

Activity 43

1. What is the difference between a fear and a phobia? Explain after finding the dictionary definitions.

_____
_____
_____

2. Make up and define your own phobia.

_____
_____
_____
_____
_____

3. What are some questions that have no right answer? List as many as you can. Pick one of the questions and try to answer it. Include what problems you have in trying to come up with a reasonable answer.

_____
_____
_____
_____

Activity 44

Personification...

What would happen if a computer could think or glasses could read?

_____
_____
_____
_____

If you could give a power to an inanimate object, what would it be and why?

_____
_____
_____
_____
_____

AND

If you could give feelings to another inanimate object, what would it say and why?

_____
_____
_____
_____
_____

Conduct Yourself...

Which are more useful? Beliefs or stereotypes?
_____
_____
_____

Which are more damaging? Beliefs or stereotypes?
_____
_____
_____

Describe situations that prove your point.
_____
_____
_____
_____
_____
_____
_____
_____

Activity 46

A Profound Perception...

"Every new idea is an impossibility until it is born."

What is the greatest invention of all time? What makes it the best?

_____
_____
_____

What is the silliest invention of all time? Why do you think it was invented?

_____
_____
_____

What would you like to invent? Why?

_____
_____
_____

Puzzles to Ponder #1...

Activity 47

Which is better...
   Giving a gift or getting one?
_____

Which is warmer...
   A hug or a cup of tea?
_____

Which is hotter...
   A new fad or an oven?
_____

Discuss your choices. Use specific examples to explain your answers.

_____
_____
_____
_____
_____
_____
_____
_____
_____

Activity 48

Puzzles to Ponder #2...

Which is tougher...
   Winning a race or eating a bad steak?
_____

Which is sharper...
   An insult or a knife?
_____

Discuss both choices. Use specific examples to explain your answers.
_____
_____
_____
_____
_____
_____

Puzzles to Ponder #3...

Activity 49

Which is slower...
   A turtle or the last 5 minutes of the school day?
_____

Which goes faster...
   A bicycle or a good book?
_____

Which has more power...
   Superman or the President?
_____

Which causes more damage...
   A hurricane or a rumor?
_____

Discuss your choices. Use specific examples to explain your answers.

_____
_____
_____
_____
_____

Activity 50

A Quick Query...

Answer each of the following questions in a separate paragraph:

1. What would happen if everyone wore the same clothes?

___

2. How would this affect how people felt about each other?

___

3. Who should decide what everyone should wear?

___

Beginnings...

Activity 51

The first sentence of a story is always the hardest.
Write a description that fits three of these "beginnings"...

- Beginning of summer vacation
- Beginning of winter
- Beginning of a new friendship
- Beginning of a new day
- Beginning of a great book
- Beginning of a new adventure
- Beginning of a batch of cookies
- Beginning of a long day of school

Describe emotions, sights, sounds, smells...
Make the reader feel the way you do about "the beginning."

_____
_____
_____
_____
_____
_____
_____
_____
_____

Activity 52

Bon Appetite...

"Don't bite off more than you can chew."

What is the most that you have ever "eaten" (literally or figuratively)?

_____
_____

Describe where, when, what, how and why!

_____
_____

How did you feel while you were eating? How did you feel after eating?

_____
_____

It takes courage to grow up and become who you really are".
Why is it so important to always be yourself?

_____
_____

In what situations is it okay to be like everyone else?

_____
_____

Explain your answers.

_____
_____

A Really Prime Number...

Activity 53

Choose one number from the number line and...

1. Tell why you chose that number...write a poem using that number.

_____
_____
_____
_____

2. In a separate paragraph, answer:

- What would happen if this number could no longer be used?

- What things begin with this number? End with this number?

- Why do you think the numbers on the number line go up in increments of 1?

- Which numbers are closest to it on the number line?

- Is there a reason why you think it is important to have this number?

- How would the number line suffer if the number was no longer there? Explain.

_____
_____
_____
_____
_____

Activity 54: A Family Affair

Your parents have told you that you need to attend a family function and you will miss school. At first you are excited but then find out that you will be missing a huge test you are prepared to take. If you don't take the test, your teacher will make you retake the test in two weeks when you are not as well prepared.

Write two paragraphs making an argument for your case to miss the trip or the test.

Consider things like: Where are you going? Who will be there? What is the significance of the trip? What will you learn? Which is more important? Which is more valuable?

_____
_____
_____
_____
_____
_____

Extension Activity: Sometimes the right thing and the appropriate thing are not the same thing. What do you think this statement means? Explain by using examples.

_____
_____
_____

Do It Yourself...

Activity 55

Write one chapter for a "Do-It-Yourself" book. Look at the titles below and choose one to write about. Illustrate your chapter with diagrams, pictures etc.

1. How to get in touch with someone from 1776.

2. How to persuade your parents to let you go on a trip with your friend's family.

3. How to influence someone to join Girl Scouts/Boy Scouts.

4. How to turn two spoons and a marshmallow into a game.

Activity 56

Impending Amazement...

Predict what transportation will be like in the year 3000.

CONSIDER: Whether it will be only cars (trucks/trains etc), what they will run on, how they will run, where they will run (road, sky etc)?

Illustrate your predictions.

_____
_____
_____
_____
_____
_____
_____
_____

What's the Point...

Activity 57

1. Why do we have schools? Write a paragraph about why schools exist.

What is good about school?
What would life be without them?
Who wants/needs them?
Is life better or worse because of them?

_____
_____
_____
_____
_____
_____

OR

2. Why do we have rules? Write a paragraph about why laws exist.

What are they good for?
How would people behave without them?
Do we need them?
Are we better or worse because of them?

_____
_____
_____
_____
_____

Activity 58
Tell Me Why...

Write a story that answers the questions...

1. Why are black cats believed to be unlucky?

_____
_____
_____
_____
_____
_____
_____

OR

2. Why are elephants believed to be afraid of mice? The last line of your story should be... "So that is why.."

_____
_____
_____
_____
_____
_____

Game On...

Activity 59

Imagine that a space alien has just landed in your backyard and wants to become your friend. You decide to break the ice by playing your favorite game. The alien can read English but cannot hear.

Your job is to teach the alien how to play the game. Use your words to describe the details and step-by-step instructions. Be VERY detailed since he has no idea what you are doing.

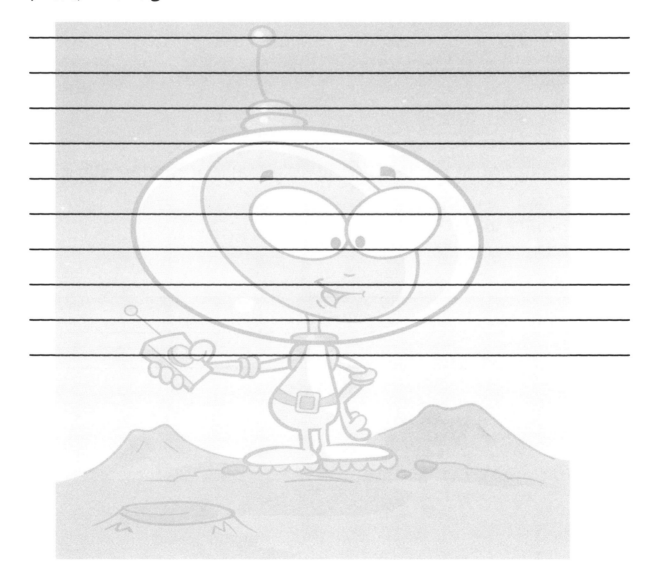

_____
_____
_____
_____
_____
_____
_____
_____
_____

Activity 60

Can I Quote You On That?

Write a creative story about:

1. The entire family sat down for their picnic in the forest. To their surprise, a bear sat down with them...

Be sure to include dialogue between the bear and the family.
(Don't forget to use quotation marks)

_____
_____
_____
_____

OR

2. The new house owner discovers a magical talking diary in the attic...
Whose diary was it?
What would the diary say?

_____
_____
_____
_____

Activity 61

Imagine This...

You are walking in the park and find a jewel encrusted box. When you open it there is a map with pictures that lead to a castle.

After giving it some thought you follow the first clue and end up in a cold, wet cave...

Conclusion: Either you are dreaming or...

Finish the story.

_____
_____
_____
_____
_____
_____
_____

Activity 62

Show Time...

If it was your job to decide which shows should be on television, which one would you choose and why?

_____
_____
_____
_____
_____
_____

Is it important to have a balance of comedy, drama, sports, cartoons, etc? Why or why not?

_____
_____
_____
_____
_____
_____

Clichés....

Activity 63

Write what you think each of these sayings mean and where they might have come from:

Be careful what you wish for...

_____
_____

Don't let the cat out of the bag...

_____
_____

Two heads are better than one...

_____
_____

Actions speak louder than words....

_____
_____

Keep your fingers crossed...

_____
_____

Activity 64

Rules and Regulations...

In school, teachers and principals are the people who make up the school rules. This is the student's chance to make up the rules of the school. You can make up rules for recess, homework, dress code, lunchtime, etc. Anything you like!

Number your rules. Be prepared to explain the need and reason for your rules.

1. _____
2. _____
3. _____
4. _____
5. _____
6. _____
7. _____
8. _____
9. _____
10. _____

How will you enforce your rules?

_____
_____

You Can't Make Me...

Activity 65

Write a sentence that will make someone:
- Feel sorry
- Laugh out loud
- Fall asleep
- Get excited

Choose your words carefully!

_____
_____
_____
_____
_____
_____
_____
_____

Activity 66

Home Sweet Home...

Think about a home that you pass by every day (one that is not your own or where you have not been inside). Concentrate on what is outside and around the home. Think about what is inside. Answer as many questions as you can in 2 separate paragraphs.

Observe:
- Who lives in the home?
- Is there only one family who lives there or are there more?
- Where is the home? Is it in a neighborhood or by itself?
- How old do you think it is? Is it new or old?
- Describe what the outside of it looks like: color, shutters/no shutters, etc.
- Do those who live there take good care of the home?
- What makes this home different than the others around it?
- Is this the kind of house that you would like to live in?

Envision:
- What types of memories do you think this house holds?
- Do you think that there are things in the attic?
- If it had a voice, do you think it could tell you stories?
- If the owners moved out, do you think that the new owners would keep it the same?
- What things could be done to the house to make it look better? Paint, landscaping, etc.
- How could you make improvements to the building?

Use your answers to draw a detailed picture of the dwelling.

Season's Greetings

Activity 67

In order to do this assignment, the class will have to be divided into groups according to their birthday season (ie. Dec., Jan., Feb. – Winter, etc).

1. With your group, think of a list of all the things you know occur during your birthday's season.
Like: celebrations, events, weather, activities, etc.

2. Your group's mission is to do the following:
   - Create a banner
   - Write a poem or jingle about your season
   - Put on a skit about your season
   - Make seasonal decorations for your part of the room

3. Provide in a rectangular cake that is plainly frosted. The group will create a design that can be put on top of a section of the cake.

4. Create seasonal costumes to wear on the day of the celebration.
   - Plan
   - Rehearse
   - Decorate Cake
   - Decorate Room
   - Present Banner/Song/Poem/Skit
   - Sing Happy Birthday
   - Cut and Eat Cake.

Activity 68

Hold Your Breath...

What would happen if everyone lived under water?
_____

Where would people live?
_____

How would children play?
_____

What would people eat?
_____

What would school be like?
_____

Would they wear bathing suits all day?
_____

Describe this under water kingdom in 2 paragraphs.
_____
_____
_____
_____

Strange Magic...

Activity 69

Your uncle is an inventor. One day you were searching in his basement for a soccer ball. To your surprise, you found a very strange machine with levers, buttons, knobs and dials. You had never seen anything like it before. On the side there is a button that says "on".

Pretend that you have pushed the button. Describe what the machine is and what it does.

_____
_____
_____
_____
_____
_____
_____
_____
_____
_____
_____
_____
_____
_____
_____

Activity 70

This or That...

Which would you rather do?

Eat or sleep _____

Swim or go camping _____

Run or walk _____

Read a book or sing a song _____

Be a rainbow or a snowflake _____

Explain your choices.

_____
_____
_____
_____
_____
_____
_____
_____
_____
_____

Tools of the Trade

Activity Pages

Write-on...

Okay, you can write (you learned how to do that back in first grade!) but one of the things that we're after this year is to make your writing interesting to read...

Some things to keep in mind as you write:

1. One of the best ways to improve the quality of your writing is to start thinking about the type of words you choose.
Some words suggest special MOODS. Usually, these kind of words are adjectives. Think before you use a word in a story.
Compare these: "The wind blew....", "The wind rattled the empty trees...", "The sun was very hot....", "The blazing sun scorched the Earth..." Ask yourself, "Is there a more descriptive way to say it?" Find these words in a thesaurus.

2. Pay attention to details, they can make things come alive.

3. Use specific examples, especially when you are trying to prove a point.

4. Try to answer these questions whenever possible: WHO, WHAT, WHY, WHERE, WHEN, HOW.

5. Describe as much as you can, in detail.

6. If possible, look at things before you write about them.... you'll be surprised at how much you can forget-- even with familiar things!

7. Feelings make writing more personal.

8. Always proofread your paper! Whenever you write something, read it over at least ONE time to be sure it sounds all right and that it makes sense. Then look for spelling and grammatical errors.

Review Page

List as many of the 8 guidelines as you can remember.

1. _____

2. _____

3. _____

4. _____

5. _____

6. _____

7. _____

8. _____

Perfect Paragraphing...

Paragraphs are used in all kinds of writing. A paragraph is a group of sentences (usually 6-8) that talks about and develops one topic.

The FIRST sentence of a paragraph is called the Topic Sentence. The Topic Sentence tells what the paragraph is going to be about.

The next few sentences develop (talk about) your topic. The sentences can be many different kinds. They can include facts or specific examples, descriptions, opinions, explanations, or incidents.

The LAST sentence of a paragraph is called the Concluding Sentence. This sentence summarizes your paragraph. You can do this by using different words to re-state your Topic Sentence.

A Sample Paragraph

indent → *topic sentence* →

    Fort River is an elementary school in Amherst, Massachusetts. The school is a one floor building with classrooms that are called "quads." Each quad has three home corners. Fort River also has a library called the Media Materials Center. The school has two cafeterias and a large gymnasium. The school was built in 1973. Fort River is one of five elementary schools in this town. ← *concluding sentence*

Review Page

Write a sample paragraph describing your school.

_____
_____
_____
_____
_____
_____
_____

After reading it over, re-write your paragraph.

_____
_____
_____
_____
_____
_____
_____

Review Page

Choose your own topic.

_____

_____

_____

_____

_____

_____

_____

Re-write

_____

_____

_____

_____

_____

_____

The Other Word...

The quality of your writing depends on the words you choose to use. Instead of always using words like "big," "small," "good," "pretty," etc., develop a vocabulary of more interesting adjectives. For the words below, find words that mean the same thing or nearly the same thing, by looking in a dictionary or thesaurus, or thinking of more interesting words yourself! Use this paper when you write.

Teacher: This assignment can be repeated often. By using different words you help your students expand their vocabulary.

GOOD
1. _____
2. _____
3. _____
4. _____

TIRED
1. _____
2. _____
3. _____
4. _____

PRETTY
1. _____
2. _____
3. _____
4. _____

BAD
1. _____
2. _____
3. _____
4. _____

NEAR
1. _____
2. _____
3. _____
4. _____

DUMB
1. _____
2. _____
3. _____
4. _____

NICE
1. _____
2. _____
3. _____
4. _____

FUN
1. _____
2. _____
3. _____
4. _____

COOL
1. _____
2. _____
3. _____
4. _____

HURT
1. _____
2. _____
3. _____
4. _____

FAR
1. _____
2. _____
3. _____
4. _____

GREAT
1. _____
2. _____
3. _____
4. _____

SMART
1. _____
2. _____
3. _____
4. _____

TERRIBLE
1. _____
2. _____
3. _____
4. _____

LONG
1. _____
2. _____
3. _____
4. _____

CRAZY
1. _____
2. _____
3. _____
4. _____

FINE
1. _____
2. _____
3. _____
4. _____

AWFUL
1. _____
2. _____
3. _____
4. _____

First Lines...
What can you tell about these stories from their first lines?

"It was a bright cold day in April, and the clocks were striking thirteen."
1984

"Crossing the lawn that morning, Douglas Spaulding broke a spider web with his face. A single invisible line on the air touched his brow and snapped without a sound."
Dandelion Wine

"A screaming comes across the sky. It has happened before, but there is nothing to compare it to now."
Gravity's Rainbow

"It was a pleasure to burn. It was a pleasure to see things eaten, to see things blackened and changed."
Fahrenheit 451

"I read about it in the paper, in the subway, on my way to work. I read it and I couldn't believe it, and I read it again."
Sonny's Blues

"Alan Austen, as nervous as a kitten, went up certain dark and creaky stairs in the neighborhood of Pell Street and peered about for a long time on the dim landing before he found the name he wanted written obscurely on one of the doors."
The Chaser

"During the whole of a dull, dark, and soundless day in the autumn of the year, when the clouds hung oppressively low in the heavens, I had been passing alone, on horseback, through a singularly dreary tract of country, and at length found myself, as the shades of the evening drew on, within view of the melancholy House of Usher."
The Fall of the House of Usher

"It was late and everyone had left the cafe except an old man who sat in the shadow the leaves of the tree made agains the electric light."
A Clean, Well-Lighted Place

"R.J. Bauman, who for fourteen years had travelled for a shoe company through Mississippi, drove his Ford along a rutted dirt path."
Death of a Salesman

"It was quite a summer. It was hot: the sun, even when it had just come up, was yellow hot and small as a quarter. There hadn't been any rain in nearly two months, and outside of town only the early cotton had come up; and the corn had rust."
The Bright Day

Sometimes first lines are very revealing about what follows, and other times they are not. That is the author's choice. Make your choices on the pages that follow.

Write an opening line for a story about:

1. A circus coming to town

_____

_____

_____

_____

2. A murder mystery

_____

_____

_____

_____

3. The first winter snowstorm

_____

_____

_____

_____

4. An incredibly hot day

_____

_____

_____

_____

5. A football game

_____

_____

_____

_____

6. A spaceship landing on the moon

_____

_____

_____

_____

7. Someone who is about to take a test he or she hasn't studied for

_____

_____

_____

_____

8. Someone who is expecting a bike for Christmas and only sees small boxes under the tree

_____

_____

_____

_____

9. A person who has to get his or her tooth pulled by a dentist

_____

_____

_____

_____

10. A child running away from home

11. Choose your own topic

12. Choose your own topic

Dynamic Workshops!

Nathan Levy is a dynamic speaker who has presented teacher, parent, and student workshops from New York to China on a wide array of topics. Nathan is a veteran educator who has taught in urban, rural, and suburban schools. He shares ways to effectively improve teaching and learning in the classroom and at home. In his role as school principal, Mr. Levy has modeled instructional leadership in an exemplary manner. Mr. Levy is the author of the famous logic series *Stories with Holes* as well as several other educational books.

The various topics for workshops which Mr. Levy presents are of great benefit to educators as well as parents. The topics focus on such areas as:

- **Critical Thinking**
- **Creativity**
- **Effective Parenting**
- **Principal Training**
- **Meeting the Standards**
- **Teaching Gifted Children**
  (in and out of the regular classrooms)
- **Reading**
- **Writing**
- **Science**
- **Differentiating Instruction**
- **Teaching Hard to Reach Learners**

Please contact us for more information about our workshops from Mr. Levy, or another of our many high caliber consultants.

Nathan Levy Books LLC

18 Moorland Blvd
Monroe Township NJ 08831

Phone 732-605-1643   Fax 732-656-7822

www.storieswithholes.com